NATIONAL GEOGRAPHIC
KiDS

Big
WORDS

FOR Little
Astronauts

The Stellar Dictionary Every
Space Explorer Needs

Lisa M. Gerry

Hi!
I'm Grover the rover,
a space exploring robot.
My mission is to guide
you through this book.
3...2...1...
Let's blast off!

NATIONAL GEOGRAPHIC
WASHINGTON, D.C.

AN ASTRO-WHAT?

Do you love space? Do you dream of visiting faraway planets? Then you're on your way to becoming an astronaut!

Astronaut ▶

(AS-truh-nawt)

An astronaut is someone who has been trained to travel beyond Earth's atmosphere into space.

Spacecraft ▶
(SPAYS-kraft)
A spacecraft is a vehicle that carries people and supplies into space.

◀ Atmosphere
(at-MUH-sfeer)
The blanket of gases that surround a planet is called the atmosphere. Earth's atmosphere has five layers.

Grover Says!

The word "astronaut" comes from the Greek words for "star sailor."

EARTH'S AWESOME ATMOSPHERE

Exosphere (Ek-soh-sfeer)

The exosphere is the last layer of the atmosphere between Earth and space. There is no air to breathe in the exosphere, and the temperature swings from very hot to very cold.

Thermosphere (THUR-muh-sfeer)

This is the hottest layer of the atmosphere. The International Space Station and many other satellites (see page 8) orbit in the thermosphere.

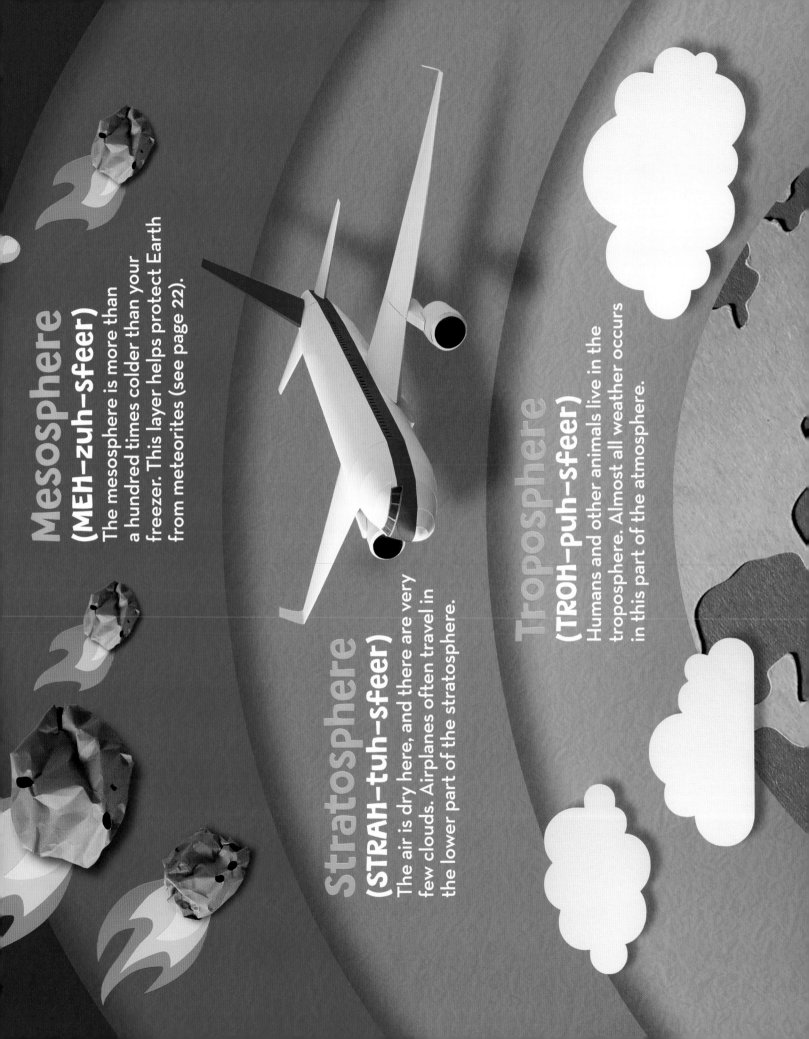

Mesosphere
(MEH–zuh–sfeer)
The mesosphere is more than a hundred times colder than your freezer. This layer helps protect Earth from meteorites (see page 22).

Stratosphere
(STRAH–tuh–sfeer)
The air is dry here, and there are very few clouds. Airplanes often travel in the lower part of the stratosphere.

Troposphere
(TROH–puh–sfeer)
Humans and other animals live in the troposphere. Almost all weather occurs in this part of the atmosphere.

SUPER-DUPER SPACE SUITS

Radiation▶
(ray-dee-AY-shun)
This is a type of energy that travels through space in waves. Too much radiation is not safe for humans, so astronauts wear protective suits. Their helmets have special gold-plated visors to protect their eyes.

◀Gravity
(GRA-vuh-tee)
Gravity is an invisible force that pulls objects toward the center of a planet. In orbit, centrifugal force (see page 30) does the opposite—it has an outward pull, so astronauts need tethers to keep from floating away.

tether

Extravehicular Mobility Units
(EK-struh-vee-HIH-kyuh-lur moh-BILL-uh-tee YOU-nits)

Extravehicular mobility units are space suits! They help protect astronauts and supply them with oxygen to breathe while exploring outside the spaceship.

▼

BLAST OFF!

How do astronauts get to space? They need the right equipment and a lot of POWER!

Orbit (OR-bit) ▶

To orbit means to move around something in a circle. For example, the moon orbits Earth, and Earth orbits the sun!

Moon

Earth

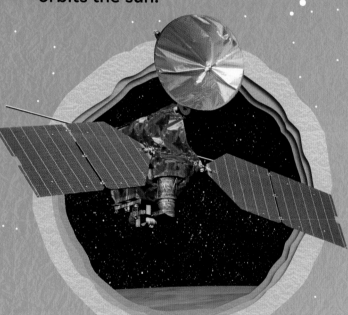

Grover Says!

Satellites help people make maps, connect cell phones, and send television signals.

Satellite (SA-tuh-lite)

A satellite is a small object that orbits a bigger object in space. Some satellites are made by people and then sent to space by rockets to orbit Earth.

Rocket (RAW-kit)

Rockets help launch a spacecraft into space. Fuel burns inside the rocket and creates hot gas that gives the spacecraft a big push! Once the spacecraft is in space, the rocket falls back down to Earth.

Propulsion (pruh-PUHL-shun)

Propulsion is the force that pushes something forward. When a spacecraft is leaving Earth's atmosphere, the rocket gives it the propulsion it needs!

INTERNATIONAL SPACE STATION

The International Space Station, or ISS, is a spacecraft that orbits Earth. Astronauts from around the world live and work on the ISS.

◀ Robonaut
(ROH-boh-nawt)
Robonauts are robots designed to look and act like human astronauts. This Robonaut, named R2, lives on the ISS. Scientists are studying it to see how it can help astronauts perform simple tasks.

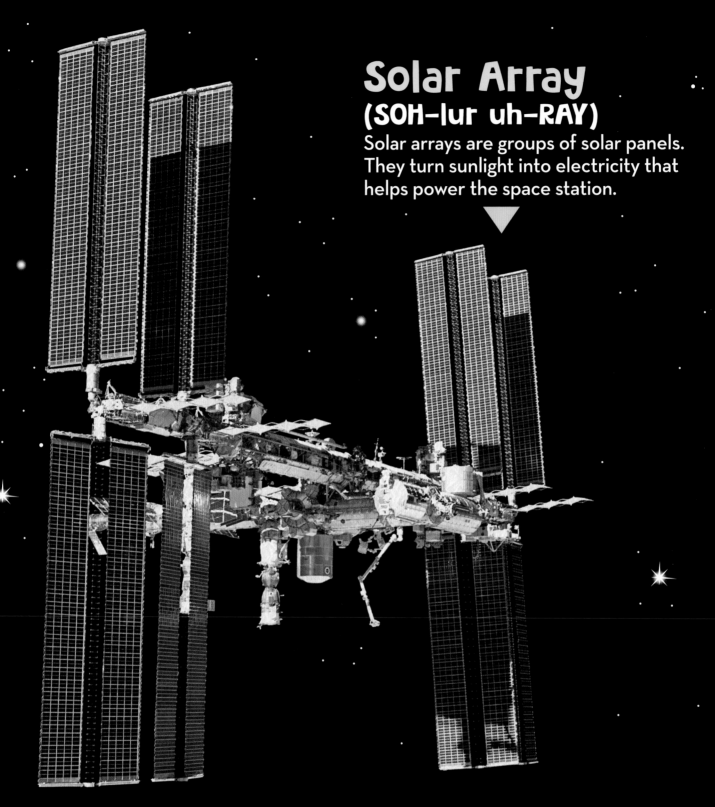

Solar Array
(SOH-lur uh-RAY)

Solar arrays are groups of solar panels. They turn sunlight into electricity that helps power the space station.

▼

◀ Cycle Ergometer
(SYE-kul err-GAH-muh-tur)

On the ISS, astronauts use this bike-like device to pedal away while staying in the same place. Astronauts must exercise for about two hours each day to keep their muscles and bones strong while in space.

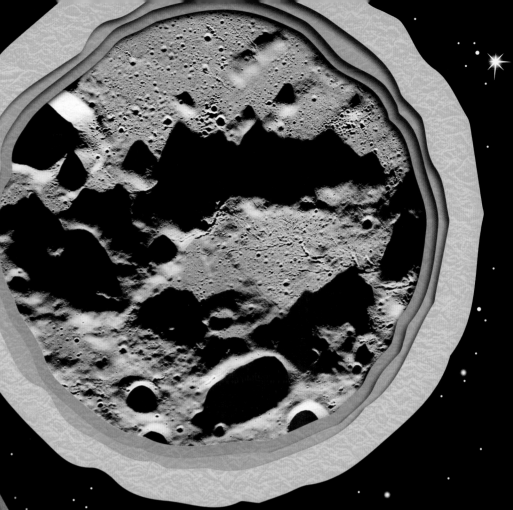

LUNAR LINGO

So far the only place in space where astronauts have landed is the moon. Would you like to visit the moon?

Lunar Maria ▶
(LOO-ner MAH-ree-uh)

The dark patches on the moon's surface are craters, or large pits, called lunar maria. They were created by asteroids (see page 22) and other space rocks crashing into the moon.

Grover Says!

The word "lunar" means having to do with the moon.

Lunar Roving Vehicle
(LOO-ner ROW-ving VEE-uh-kul)
Astronauts traveled on the moon's surface in a lunar roving vehicle, also called a moon buggy.

Lunar Module ▲
(LOO-ner MAH-jool)
The lunar module was the part of the spacecraft that astronauts used to land on the moon.

Regolith
(RAY-guh-lith)
Regolith is loose, crumbly soil mixed with bits of rocks, minerals, and even glass. The surface of the moon is covered in regolith.

HEADING HOME

Brace yourself as your spacecraft returns to Earth!

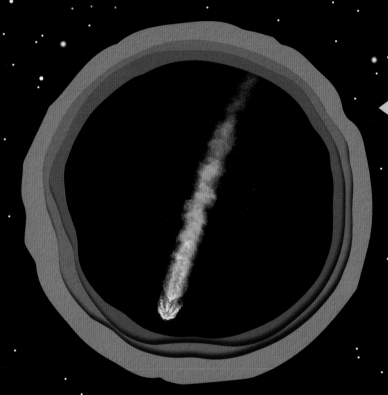

◀ Hypersonic
(HIGH–pur–SAHN–ik)

Hypersonic speed means traveling more than five times the speed of sound. A spacecraft reentering Earth's atmosphere travels at hypersonic speed.

Trajectory ▶
(truh–JEK–tuh–ree)

The path of an object in motion is called its trajectory. A spacecraft uses a curved trajectory both to leave Earth's orbit, shown here, and to return to Earth.

Parachute
(PARE-uh-shoot)

As a returning spacecraft gets closer to Earth's surface, it will often use one or more parachutes to help it slow down for a softer landing.

Splashdown
(SPLASH-down)

Sometimes a returning spacecraft will land in a body of water. This is called a splashdown. Once the spacecraft is in the water, large ships and helicopters help find it and pull it out safely.

EARTH'S SOLAR SYSTEM

Our solar system is made up of the sun and all the planets and other objects that orbit it.

Mars
(MARZ)

Mercury
(MUR-kyuh-ree)

Earth
(URTH)

Venus
(VEE-nuhs)

Sun
(SUN)

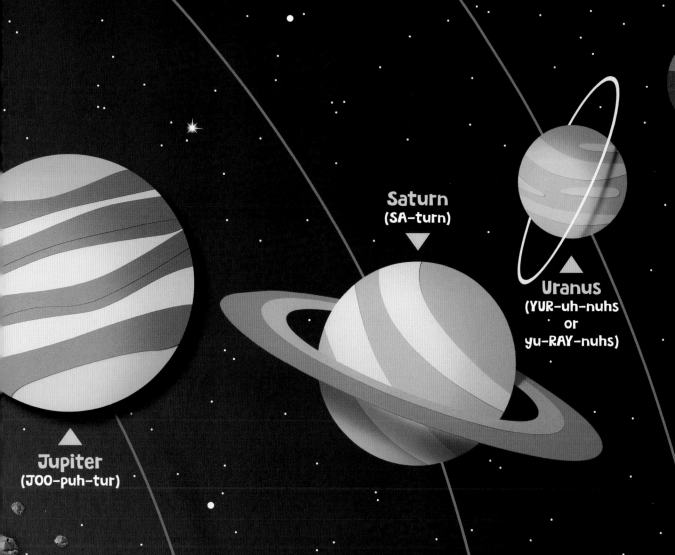

Saturn
(SA–turn)

Neptune
(NEP–toon)

Uranus
(YUR–uh–nuhs
or
yu–RAY–nuhs)

Jupiter
(JOO–puh–tur)

Heliocentric
(HEE–lee–oh–SEN–trik)
Earth's solar system is heliocentric.
This means the sun is at the center.

◀ asteroid belt

MORE SOLAR SYSTEM STUFF

Kuiper Belt
(KY-pur BELT)

This doughnut-shaped area of space lies past the planet Neptune. It is where you can find the smallest planets in our solar system, called dwarf planets.

Pluto ▶
(PLOO–toe)

Pluto was once considered the ninth planet in our solar system. Then, in 2006, scientists decided it was too small to be a planet. Now Pluto is considered a dwarf planet in the Kuiper Belt.

◀Haumea
(how–MEH–ya)

Haumea is another dwarf planet in the Kuiper Belt. It is about the same size as Pluto, but Haumea is shaped like an egg!

Grover Says!

Who named Pluto? An 11-year-old girl from England! Do you have ideas for planet names?

19

CLOSE-UP: MARS

Mars is known as the red planet. Humans haven't visited Mars yet, but robots (like rovers!) have.

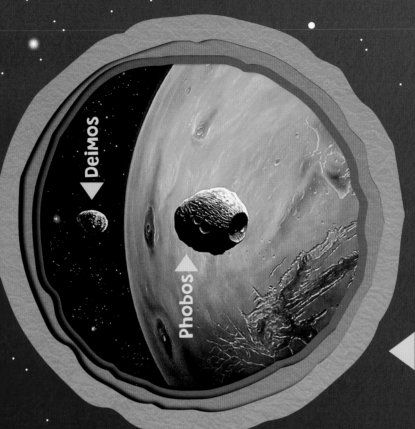

Deimos

Phobos

Mars Reconnaissance Orbiter
(MARZ reh-KAH-neh-zents OR-beh-tur)

The Mars Reconnaissance Orbiter is a spacecraft that has been traveling around Mars for almost 20 years. It takes photos and collects information about the planet and then sends it all back to Earth.

Phobos and Deimos
(FOE-bose) (DEE-mose)

Mars has two bumpy moons. Phobos is the largest and stays closer to the planet, while Deimos is smaller and farther away.

Spirit and Opportunity
(SPEER-it)
(AH-pur-TOO-nuh-tee)

Spirit and Opportunity, nicknamed "the adventure twins," were two rovers sent to Mars to explore its surface. Each one weighed about 400 pounds (181 kg). For years, they sent information about their discoveries back to Earth.

FLYING FIERY SPACE ROCKS!

The universe is abuzz with whizzing, whirring, barreling, bursting space objects!

Asteroid ▶
(AH-stuh-royd)

This is a rocky object that orbits the sun. Some asteroids are smooth and round like a ball, but most are jagged and have pits and craters on their surfaces.

◀ Meteorite
(MEE-tee-uh-rite)

A chunk of space rock, or meteor, that reaches Earth's surface is called a meteorite. Most meteorites are small enough to fit in your hand.

Meteor
(MEE-tee-or)

Meteors are chunks of space rock that never reach Earth's surface. They burn as they pass through Earth's atmosphere. This creates a flash of light, which some people call a shooting star.

Comet
(KAH-muht)

Comets orbit the sun just like asteroids, but they are mostly frozen water or gas. Comets are nicknamed "dirty snowballs."

Grover Says!

Astronomers have observed more than 3,900 comets orbiting the sun.

WEIRD, WILD WONDERS

These magnificent marvels are truly out of this world!

Cryovolcano
(KRYE-oh-vahl-KAY-noh)

A cryovolcano is a volcano that erupts ice and water rather than lava. Cryovolcanoes have been found on Enceladus, one of Saturn's 146 moons.

▼

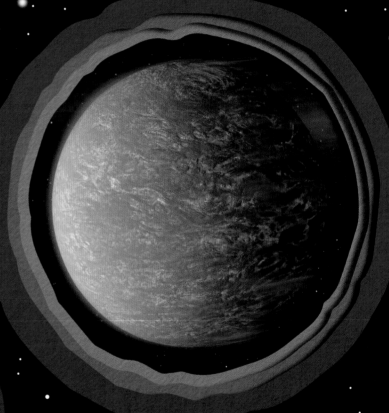

▲

55 Cancri e
(FIF-tee-FIVE KAN-kree EE)

This planet orbits a nearby star in the Milky Way galaxy (see page 27). Experts believe it is covered in lava!

Nebula
(NEH-byuh-luh)

When certain stars lose energy, they explode. All the leftover stardust is called a nebula. Gases and dust can also come together to form new stars within nebulas.

STAR POWER

The night sky sparkles with these twinkly lights. What are stars? They are large, glowing balls of gases.

◀ Constellation
(kont-stuh-LAY-shun)

A constellation is a group of stars that has been given a name based on something it looks like. For example, the constellation Orion is said to look like a hunter with a sword.

Supernova ▶
(soo-pur-NOH-vuh)

When some stars reach the end of their life, they explode in an enormous blast of light. This is called a supernova.

Galaxy
(GAH-lek-see)

A galaxy is a huge group of stars, solar systems, gas, and dust—all held together by gravity. Earth's solar system is part of the Milky Way galaxy.

Grover Says!

Scientists think there may be up to two TRILLION galaxies in our universe.

STUDYING SPACE FROM EARTH

There are plenty of ways to explore space right here on Earth!

Telescope
(TEH-leh-skope)

A telescope is a tool that lets you see faraway objects, like the moon and stars. ▼

Astronomer
(uh–STRAH–nuh–mer)

An astronomer is someone who studies everything outside of Earth's atmosphere, including the sun, planets, moons, and stars.

Astrophotographer ▶
(ah–stroh–fuh–TAH–gruh–fur)

An astrophotographer is someone who takes pictures of objects and events in space.

Observatory
(ub–ZER–vuh–tore–ee) ▼

Observatories are special buildings for studying space. They are equipped with very powerful telescopes.

MORE BIG WORDS

Aurora
(uh-ROHR-uh)
Auroras are glowing streams of colored light sometimes seen in the night sky. They happen when particles from the sun enter Earth's atmosphere.

Betelgeuse
(BEE-tuhl-joos)
This supergiant star is about 700 times the size of the sun. Betelgeuse is one of the easiest stars to see from Earth without needing a telescope.

Centrifugal Force
(sen-TRIF-yuh-guhl FORS)
When an object is moving quickly around in a circle, like in orbit, it tends to move outward from the center. This special energy is centrifugal force.

Extraterrestrial
(ek-struh-tuh-REH-stree-uhl)
Extraterrestrial means anything outside of Earth and its atmosphere.

Intergalactic
(in-tur-guh-LAK-tik)
The space between galaxies is called intergalactic space.

Noctilucent Clouds
(nahk-tuh-LOO-sent KLOWDS)
These wispy clouds form way up in the mesosphere. Noctilucent clouds are rare and can only be seen from Earth under special conditions after sunset.

Oxygen (AWK-suh-jen)
Oxygen is a gas that almost all living things need to survive. There's not much oxygen in space, so astronauts get the oxygen they need from tanks in their space suit or spacecraft.

Planetesimal
(pla-neh-TEH-sih-mul)
A planetesimal is a small rocky body that orbits a star. It may become a planet by drawing in more material.

Universe (YOU-nuh-vers)
The universe includes everything that exists, everywhere—our solar system, the galaxies, all of space, everything! Earth and we humans who live here are just a teeny tiny part of the universe.

Grover Says!

Looking for a challenge? Let's see if you can master these stellar space words!

For my mom, Gail, who knows all the best big words and who I love more than there are stars in the sky. —L.M.G.

NATIONAL GEOGRAPHIC and Yellow Border Design are trademarks of the National Geographic Society, used under license.

Since 1888, the National Geographic Society has funded more than 14,000 research, conservation, education, and storytelling projects around the world. National Geographic Partners distributes a portion of the funds it receives from your purchase to National Geographic Society to support programs including the conservation of animals and their habitats. To learn more, visit natgeo.com/info.

For more information, visit nationalgeographic.com, call 1-877-873-6846, or write to the following address:

National Geographic Partners, LLC
1145 17th Street NW
Washington, DC 20036-4688 U.S.A.

More for kids from National Geographic: natgeokids.com

National Geographic Kids magazine inspires children to explore their world with fun yet educational articles on animals, science, nature, and more. Using fresh storytelling and amazing photography, *Nat Geo Kids* shows kids ages 6 to 14 the fascinating truth about the world—and why they should care. **natgeo.com/subscribe**

For rights or permissions inquiries, please contact National Geographic Books Subsidiary Rights: bookrights@natgeo.com

Designed by Brett Challos

The publisher would like to thank Kathryn Sullivan, PhD, former NASA astronaut, for her expert review of this book; Maren Schabhüser, paper artist, for creating Grover the rover; and Katherine Kling, fact-checker. Book team: Lori Epstein, photo manager; Sarah Gardner, associate photo editor; Emily Fego, project editor; Molly Reid, production editor; and Lauren Sciortino and David Marvin, associate designers.

Hardcover ISBN: 978-1-4263-7644-3
Reinforced library binding ISBN: 978-1-4263-7646-7

Printed in China
24/LPC/1

Photo Credits

All cut paper artwork of rover, astronaut, satellites, asteroids, and flames by Maren Schabhüser/Mendola Ltd.; Cover: (shuttle) 3DSulptor/Adobe Stock; (Mars) Everest Arts/Shutterstock; (Earth) pio3/Shutterstock; (galaxy) Swardian/Shutterstock; Cover front flap: (speech bubble), Roman Yaroshchuk/Adobe Stock, (BACKGROUND), Ninja Artist/Shutterstock; speech bubble, (throughout) Roman Yaroshchuk/Adobe Stock; white paper texture (throughout), Ninja Artist/Shutterstock; 1, Swardian/Shutterstock; 2-3, Heidemarie M. Stefanyshyn-Piper/NASA; 2, studio023/Adobe Stock; 3, 3DSulptor/Adobe Stock; 6 (UP), Arthur de Wolf/NASA; 6 (LO), JSC/NASA; 6-7, NASA; 8 (LE), JPL/NASA; 8 (RT), Johan Swanepoel/Adobe Stock; 9, MSFC/NASA; 10 (UP), NASA; 10 (LO), NASA; 10-11, NASA/Associated Press; 12, JSC/NASA; 13, JSC/NASA; 14 (UP), SPACEX/Science Source; 14 (LO), Joel Kowsky/NASA; 15, Bill Ingalls/NASA/AP Photo; 18, Nicolle R. Fuller/Science Source; 19 (UP), Aphelleon/Shutterstock; 19 (LO), David Aguilar/National Geographic Society; 20, David A. Hardy/Science Source; 20-21, JPL/NASA; 21, NASA; 22 (UP), vencav/Adobe Stock; 22 (LO), nuttapongg/Adobe Stock; 23 (UP), NASA Image Collection/Alamy Stock Photo; 23 (BACKGROUND), Jasmine_K/Shutterstock; 24 (UP), JPL/NASA; 24 (LO), Ron Miller/Science Source; 25, Beginning_artist/Shutterstock; 26 (UP), vchalup/Adobe Stock; 26 (LO), JPL/NASA; 26-27 (BACKGROUND), Loren Gosselin/Wirestock Creators/Adobe Stock; 28 (BACKGROUND), Babak Tefreshi/National Geographic Image Collection; 28 (LO), allexxandarx/Adobe Stock; 29 (UP), Babak Tafreshi/National Geographic Image Collection; 29 (CTR), Babak Tafreshi; 29 (LO), Babak Tafreshi/National Geographic Image Collection; 30, Ralph Lee Hopkins/National Geographic Image Collection; 31, Jan Erik Paulsen/NASA

While we strive to show objects in space as accurately as possible, the relative distance between objects is not to scale.

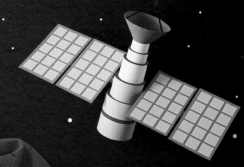